Speak, Lord, I am Listening

A Scriptural Rosary Book by Christine Haapala
Illustrated by Gus Muller

Suffering Servant Scriptorium
Fairfax, Virginia

www.sufferingservant.com

Published with Ecclesiastical Permission
Diocese of Arlington
February 14, 2001

Verse text from the *New American Bible with Revised New Testament and Psalm* Copyright © 1991, 1986, 1970 by the Confraternity of Christian Doctrine, Washington, D.C. Used with permission. All Rights Reserved. No part of the *New American Bible* may be reproduced in any form without permission in writing from the copyright owner.

<u>Speak, Lord, I am Listening</u>, 1st edition, Watercolor Illustrations, Copyright © 2001, 2004, 2011 Gus Muller; Luminous Mystery Watercolor Illustrations © 2004, 2011 Gus Muller

Copyright © 2001, 2004, 2011 Christine Haapala
All Rights Reserved.

ISBN 13: 978-0-9703996-7-0; ISBN 10: 0-9703996-7-7; The Joyful, Sorrowful, and Glorious Mysteries of the Most Holy Rosary first appeared in <u>Speak, Lord, I am Listening</u> (First Edition, ISBN 0-9703996-2-6)

2nd Edition: Design Layout by Alison Ujueta.

2nd Edition: Fourth printing, 2011.

Manufactured in the United States of America

Dedicated to
the Blessed Virgin Mary, Our Lady of Fatima

Special thanks to Father Michael Duesterhaus
for his spiritual direction and encouragement.

The printing of this edition was made possible through the generosity of Alice Anne Walecka, widow of Norman "Wally" Walecka. May he rest in peace and may perpetual light shine on him. Alice is the mother of 5, grandmother of 7, and great-grandmother of 5.

Children too are a gift from the LORD. *Psalm 127:3*

Letter to Parents

Dear Parents,

This book was written to assist you in your role as "first teachers of your child in faith." (from the Rite of Baptism). Children practice on musical instruments when they are young so that they are proficient when they grow up; they practice playing sports so as to grow in skill, so with prayer. By beginning their life of faith early children come to appreciate and develop a relationship with God. Whether your child is preparing for First Holy Communion, or you are using this book with a younger child as part of a family time of prayer, no effort to raise a child in the vocabulary of faith will be wanting.

Often there are objections, by both adult and child alike, to praying the Most Holy Rosary. These are easily addressed:

- The Rosary is too long.
  Then start with one decade at a time.

- The Rosary is too repetitive, too boring.
  Then intertwine Scripture verses with the prayers.

- The Rosary is only prayed by old people.
  If only we could pray like Mother Teresa did.
  (When did old people start praying the rosary? As little children!)

- There is not enough time to pray the Rosary.
  What is more important, a television show or our relationship with God?

- There are too many distractions when praying the Rosary.
  Then don't pray alone; pray with family and friends to keep on track.

- I don't understand the Mysteries.
  Again, use the Scriptures listed with each of the mysteries as a link to the Bible to find out more.

- I've never prayed the Rosary, so how can I teach my kids?
  Just Do It (to borrow a phrase) and learn together.

- There are too many more fun things to do than to take time to pray the Rosary.
  Our life in eternity begins now in little opportunities of sacrifice for God.

- I do not know anyone else who prays the Rosary.
  Get to know St. Dominic, St. Elizabeth Ann Seton, St. John Neumann, St. Katherine Drexel, St. Maximilian Kolbe, St. Edith Stein, and, of course, Pope Blessed John Paul II.

- So what is the big deal about Mary and the Rosary?
  Mary is the Mother of God. What other person has such a great title and honor?

May the Blessed Mother lead you and your child closer to her Son, Jesus Christ, for that is why she was given to us by Him.

Fr. Michael R. Duesterhaus
PRIEST OF THE DIOCESE OF ARLINGTON, VA

Table of Contents

Letter to Parents iv

Speak, Lord, I am Listening A Scriptural Rosary 1

The Joyful Mysteries 2
    The Annunciation 4
    The Visitation 6
    The Nativity 8
    The Presentation of Jesus in the Temple 10
    The Finding of Jesus in the Temple 12

The Luminous Mysteries 14
    The Baptism of Jesus 16
    The Wedding at Cana 18
    The Proclamation of the Kingdom 20
    The Transfiguration 22
    The Institution of the Eucharist 24

The Sorrowful Mysteries 26
    The Agony in the Garden 28
    The Scourging at the Pillar 30
    The Crowning of Thorns 32
    The Carrying of the Cross 34
    The Crucifixion 36

The Glorious Mysteries 38
    The Resurrection 40
    The Ascension 42
    The Descent of the Holy Spirit 44
    The Assumption of the Blessed Virgin Mary
        into Heaven 46
    The Coronation of the Blessed Virgin Mary,
        Queen of Heaven and Earth 48

The Books of the Bible 50
Frequently Asked Questions 51
Study and Discussion Guide 54
Other Titles Available from *Suffering Servant Scriptorium* 58

Speak, Lord, I am Listening

A Scriptural Rosary Book

The Joyful Mysteries

In the Name of the Father and of the Son and of the Holy Spirit. Amen.

I believe in God, the Father almighty, Creator of heaven and earth, and in Jesus Christ, his only Son, our Lord, who was conceived by the Holy Spirit, born of the Virgin Mary, suffered under Pontius Pilate, was crucified, died and was buried; he descended into hell; on the third day he rose again from the dead; he ascended into heaven, and is seated at the right hand of God the Father almighty; from there he will come to judge the living and the dead. I believe in the Holy Spirit, the holy catholic Church, the communion of saints, the forgiveness of sins, the resurrection of the body, and life everlasting. Amen.

"Speak, for your servant is listening."

1 Samuel 3:10

Our Father, Who art in Heaven, hallowed be Thy Name. Thy kingdom come, Thy will be done on earth as it is in Heaven. Give us this day our daily bread, and forgive us our trespasses, as we forgive those who trespass against us. And lead us not into temptation, but deliver us from evil. Amen.

"Have faith in God." *Mark 11:22*

Hail Mary, full of grace, the Lord is with thee; blessed art thou among women, and blessed is the Fruit of thy womb, Jesus. Holy Mary, Mother of God, pray for us sinners, now and at the hour of our death. Amen.

I put my hope in your word. *Psalm 119:81*

Hail Mary …

God is love.
1 John 4:8

Hail Mary …

Glory be to the Father, and to the Son, and to the Holy Spirit. As it was in the beginning, is now, and ever shall be, world without end. Amen.

The First Joyful Mystery
The Annunciation

Bless the LORD, all you angels.
Psalm 103:20

Our Father, Who art in Heaven, hallowed be Thy Name. Thy kingdom come, Thy will be done on earth as it is in Heaven. Give us this day our daily bread, and forgive us our trespasses, as we forgive those who trespass against us. And lead us not into temptation, but deliver us from evil. Amen.

Before I formed you in the womb I knew you. Jeremiah 1:5

Hail Mary, full of grace, the Lord is with thee; blessed art thou among women, and blessed is the Fruit of thy womb, Jesus. Holy Mary, Mother of God, pray for us sinners, now and at the hour of our death. Amen.

You formed my inmost being; ... so wonderfully you made me. Psalm 139:13-14

Hail Mary ...

The angel Gabriel was sent from God.
Luke 1:26

Hail Mary ...

O most beautiful among women. *Song of Songs 1:8*

Hail Mary ...

The virgin's name was Mary. ... Choose life. *Luke 1:27, Deuteronomy 30:19*

Hail Mary ...

"The child to be born will be called holy, the Son of God." ... Immanuel. *Luke 1:35, Isaiah 7:14*

Hail Mary ...

Mary said, "Behold, I am the handmaid of the Lord." *Luke 1:38*

Hail Mary ...

I will praise you, LORD, with all my heart. *Psalm 9:2*

Hail Mary ...

"Blessed is the fruit of your womb." ... Jesus

Luke 1:42, Matthew 1:21

Hail Mary ...

Blessed is the man who trusts in the LORD. *Jeremiah 17:7*

Hail Mary ...

Glory be to the Father, and to the Son, and to the Holy Spirit. As it was in the beginning, is now, and ever shall be, world without end. Amen.

O My Jesus, forgive us our sins, save us from the fires of Hell, lead all souls to Heaven, especially those who are in most need of Thy Mercy.

The Second Joyful Mystery
The Visitation

Show me the path I should walk, for to you I entrust my life.
Psalm 143:8

Our Father, Who art in Heaven, hallowed be Thy Name. Thy kingdom come, Thy will be done on earth as it is in Heaven. Give us this day our daily bread, and forgive us our trespasses, as we forgive those who trespass against us. And lead us not into temptation, but deliver us from evil. Amen.

"Do not fear ... your God, is with you wherever you go." *Joshua 1:9*

Hail Mary, full of grace, the Lord is with thee; blessed art thou among women, and blessed is the Fruit of thy womb, Jesus. Holy Mary, Mother of God, pray for us sinners, now and at the hour of our death. Amen.

Children too are a gift from the LORD.
Psalm 127:3

Hail Mary ...

"Zechariah, ... Your wife Elizabeth will bear you a son ... John." *Luke 1:13*

Hail Mary ...

Mary set out ... in haste to a town of Judah. *Luke 1:39*

Hail Mary ...

May your faithful ones rejoice in good things. *2 Chronicles 6:41*

Hail Mary ...

When Elizabeth heard Mary's greeting, the infant leaped in her womb. *Luke 1:41*

Hail Mary ...

Mary said: "My soul proclaims the greatness of the Lord." *Luke 1:46*

Hail Mary …

Serve one another through love. *Galatians 5:13*

Hail Mary …

Mary remained with [Elizabeth] about three months. *Luke 1:56*

Hail Mary …

If we love one another, God remains in us. *1 John 4:12*

Hail Mary …

Glory be to the Father, and to the Son, and to the Holy Spirit. As it was in the beginning, is now, and ever shall be, world without end. Amen.

O My Jesus, forgive us our sins, save us from the fires of Hell, lead all souls to Heaven, especially those who are in most need of Thy Mercy.

The Third Joyful Mystery
The Nativity

Blow the trumpet in Zion … the day of the LORD is coming. *Joel 2:1*

Our Father, Who art in Heaven, hallowed be Thy Name. Thy kingdom come, Thy will be done on earth as it is in Heaven. Give us this day our daily bread, and forgive us our trespasses, as we forgive those who trespass against us. And lead us not into temptation, but deliver us from evil. Amen.

I am coming to dwell among you, says the LORD. *Zechariah 2:14*

Hail Mary, full of grace, the Lord is with thee; blessed art thou among women, and blessed is the Fruit of thy womb, Jesus. Holy Mary, Mother of God, pray for us sinners, now and at the hour of our death. Amen.

Joseph … was of the house and family of David. *Luke 2:4*

Hail Mary …

[Mary] gave birth to her firstborn son … and laid him in a manger. *Luke 2:7*

Hail Mary …

A child is born to us. … Prince of Peace.
Isaiah 9:5

Hail Mary …

The Shepherds said, … "Let us go, then to Bethlehem." *Luke 2:15*

Hail Mary …

"We saw his star." … [The magi] offered him gifts of gold, frankincense and myrrh.
Matthew 2:2,11

Hail Mary …

We saw his glory, the glory as of the Father's only Son.

John 1:14

Hail Mary ...

He is the Son of God. *John 1:34*

Hail Mary ...

At the name of Jesus every knee should bend.

Philippians 2:10

Hail Mary ...

Jesus said ... "Do you love me?" *John 21:15-16*

Hail Mary ...

Glory be to the Father, and to the Son, and to the Holy Spirit. As it was in the beginning, is now, and ever shall be, world without end. Amen.

O My Jesus, forgive us our sins, save us from the fires of Hell, lead all souls to Heaven, especially those who are in most need of Thy Mercy.

The Fourth Joyful Mystery
The Presentation of Jesus in the Temple

We have agreed to bring each year to the house of the LORD ... the first-born of our children. *Nehemiah 10:36-37*

Our Father, Who art in Heaven, hallowed be Thy Name. Thy kingdom come, Thy will be done on earth as it is in Heaven. Give us this day our daily bread, and forgive us our trespasses, as we forgive those who trespass against us. And lead us not into temptation, but deliver us from evil. Amen.

Be firm and steadfast, taking care to observe the entire law. *Joshua 1:7*

Hail Mary, full of grace, the Lord is with thee; blessed art thou among women, and blessed is the Fruit of thy womb, Jesus. Holy Mary, Mother of God, pray for us sinners, now and at the hour of our death. Amen.

Perfect wisdom is the fulfillment of the law. *Sirach 19:17*

Hail Mary ...

Priests of the Lord, bless the Lord. *Daniel 3:84*

Hail Mary ...

When the parents brought in the child Jesus, [Simeon said], ... "my eyes have seen your salvation." *Luke 2:27,30*

Hail Mary ...

Sing his praises in Jerusalem.
Tobit 13:8

Hail Mary ...

A prophetess, Anna, ... gave thanks to God. *Luke 2:36,38*

Hail Mary ...

[Jesus] grew and became strong, filled with wisdom. *Luke 2:40*

Hail Mary ...

Whoever is wise, stay close to him.
Sirach 6:34

Hail Mary ...

The love of God has been poured into our hearts. *Romans 5:5*

Hail Mary ...

His mother kept all these things in her heart. *Luke 2:51*

Hail Mary ...

Glory be to the Father, and to the Son, and to the Holy Spirit. As it was in the beginning, is now, and ever shall be, world without end. Amen.

O My Jesus, forgive us our sins, save us from the fires of Hell, lead all souls to Heaven, especially those who are in most need of Thy Mercy.

The Fifth Joyful Mystery
The Finding of Jesus in the Temple

You shall seek the LORD, your God. *Deuteronomy 4:29*

Our Father, Who art in Heaven, hallowed be Thy Name. Thy kingdom come, Thy will be done on earth as it is in Heaven. Give us this day our daily bread, and forgive us our trespasses, as we forgive those who trespass against us. And lead us not into temptation, but deliver us from evil. Amen.

Those who seek me find me. *Proverbs 8:17*

Hail Mary, full of grace, the Lord is with thee; blessed art thou among women, and blessed is the Fruit of thy womb, Jesus. Holy Mary, Mother of God, pray for us sinners, now and at the hour of our death. Amen.

After three days, [Joseph and Mary] found him in the temple. *Luke 2:46*

Hail Mary …

[Jesus was] sitting in the midst of the teachers, listening to them and asking them questions. *Luke 2:46*

Hail Mary …

Your teaching is my delight. *Psalm 119:174*

Hail Mary …

How I love your teaching, Lord! I study it all day long. *Psalm 119:97*

Hail Mary …

He said to them, "… Did you not know I must be in my Father's house." *Luke 2:49*

Hail Mary …

Peoples will speak of his wisdom. *Sirach 39:10*

Hail Mary ...

Whoever remains in the teaching has the Father and the Son. *2 John 9*

Hail Mary ...

[Jesus] came to Nazareth, and was obedient to them. *Luke 2:51*

Hail Mary ...

Children, obey your parents [in the Lord], for this is right. *Ephesians 6:1*

Hail Mary ...

Glory be to the Father, and to the Son, and to the Holy Spirit. As it was in the beginning, is now, and ever shall be, world without end. Amen.

O My Jesus, forgive us our sins, save us from the fires of Hell, lead all souls to Heaven, especially those who are in most need of Thy Mercy.

Hail, holy Queen, Mother of mercy, our life, our sweetness and our hope. To thee do we cry, poor banished children of Eve! To thee do we send up our sighs, mourning and weeping in this valley of tears. Turn then, most gracious advocate, thine eyes of mercy towards us. And after this, our exile, show unto us the blessed Fruit of thy womb, Jesus. O clement, O loving, O sweet Virgin Mary.

V. Pray for us, O holy Mother of God,
R. That we may be made worthy of the promises of Christ.

The Luminous Mysteries

In the Name of the Father and of the Son and of the Holy Spirit. Amen.

I believe in God, the Father almighty, Creator of heaven and earth, and in Jesus Christ, his only Son, our Lord, who was conceived by the Holy Spirit, born of the Virgin Mary, suffered under Pontius Pilate, was crucified, died and was buried; he descended into hell; on the third day he rose again from the dead; he ascended into heaven, and is seated at the right hand of God the Father almighty; from there he will come to judge the living and the dead. I believe in the Holy Spirit, the holy catholic Church, the communion of saints, the forgiveness of sins, the resurrection of the body, and life everlasting. Amen.

God is light. ... Live as children of light.

1 John 1:5, Ephesians 5:8

Our Father, Who art in Heaven, hallowed be Thy Name. Thy kingdom come, Thy will be done on earth as it is in Heaven. Give us this day our daily bread, and forgive us our trespasses, as we forgive those who trespass against us. And lead us not into temptation, but deliver us from evil. Amen.

"Everything is possible to one who has faith." *Mark 9:23*

Hail Mary, full of grace, the Lord is with thee; blessed art thou among women, and blessed is the Fruit of thy womb, Jesus. Holy Mary, Mother of God, pray for us sinners, now and at the hour of our death. Amen.

Make straight your ways and hope in him.
Sirach 2:6

Hail Mary ...

Whoever loves his brother remains in the light. *1 John 2:10*

Hail Mary ...

Glory be to the Father, and to the Son, and to the Holy Spirit. As it was in the beginning, is now, and ever shall be, world without end. Amen.

The First Luminous Mystery
The Baptism of Jesus

"You will go before the Lord to prepare his ways." *Luke 1:76*

Our Father, Who art in Heaven, hallowed be Thy Name. Thy kingdom come, Thy will be done on earth as it is in Heaven. Give us this day our daily bread, and forgive us our trespasses, as we forgive those who trespass against us. And lead us not into temptation, but deliver us from evil. Amen.

John the Baptist appeared in the desert. *Mark 1:4*

Hail Mary, full of grace, the Lord is with thee; blessed art thou among women, and blessed is the Fruit of thy womb, Jesus. Holy Mary, Mother of God, pray for us sinners, now and at the hour of our death. Amen.

Jesus came from Galilee to John at the Jordan to be baptized. *Matthew 3:13*

Hail Mary ...

"Behold, the Lamb of God, who takes away the sin of the world." *John 1:29*

Hail Mary ...

"I saw the Spirit come down like a dove." *John 1:32*

Hail Mary ...

A voice came from the heavens. *Matthew 3:17*

Hail Mary ...

"This is my beloved Son, with whom I am pleased." *Matthew 3:17*

Hail Mary ...

One Lord, one faith, one baptism; one God and Father of all.

Ephesians 4:5-6

Hail Mary ...

I will sprinkle clean water upon you. *Ezekiel 36:25*

Hail Mary ...

Cleanse me ... that I may be pure. *Psalm 51:9*

Hail Mary ...

Make disciples of all nations, baptizing them in the name of the Father, and of the Son, and of the holy Spirit. *Matthew 28:19*

Hail Mary ...

Glory be to the Father, and to the Son, and to the Holy Spirit. As it was in the beginning, is now, and ever shall be, world without end. Amen.

O My Jesus, forgive us our sins, save us from the fires of Hell, lead all souls to Heaven, especially those who are in most need of Thy Mercy.

The Second Luminous Mystery
The Wedding at Cana

Let marriage be honored among all.

Hebrews 13:4

Our Father, Who art in Heaven, hallowed be Thy Name. Thy kingdom come, Thy will be done on earth as it is in Heaven. Give us this day our daily bread, and forgive us our trespasses, as we forgive those who trespass against us. And lead us not into temptation, but deliver us from evil. Amen.

There was a wedding in Cana in Galilee. *John 2:1*

Hail Mary, full of grace, the Lord is with thee; blessed art thou among women, and blessed is the Fruit of thy womb, Jesus. Holy Mary, Mother of God, pray for us sinners, now and at the hour of our death. Amen.

The bridegroom came and those who were ready went into the wedding feast. *Matthew 25:10*

Hail Mary ...

The mother of Jesus was there.
John 2:1

Hail Mary ...

The mother of Jesus said to him, "They have no wine." *John 2:3*

Hail Mary ...

"Woman, how does your concern affect me? My hour has not yet come." *John 2:4*

Hail Mary ...

His mother said ... "Do whatever he tells you." *John 2:5*

Hail Mary ...

"You have kept the good wine until now." *John 2:10*

Hail Mary ...

Jesus did this as the beginning of his signs. *John 2:11*

Hail Mary ...

"Believe me that I am in the Father and the Father is in me." *John 14:11*

Hail Mary ...

His disciples began to believe in him. *John 2:11*

Hail Mary ...

Glory be to the Father, and to the Son, and to the Holy Spirit. As it was in the beginning, is now, and ever shall be, world without end. Amen.

O My Jesus, forgive us our sins, save us from the fires of Hell, lead all souls to Heaven, especially those who are in most need of Thy Mercy.

The Third Luminous Mystery
The Proclamation of the Kingdom

Jesus began to preach and say, "Repent, for the kingdom of heaven is at hand." *Matthew 4:17*

Our Father, Who art in Heaven, hallowed be Thy Name. Thy kingdom come, Thy will be done on earth as it is in Heaven. Give us this day our daily bread, and forgive us our trespasses, as we forgive those who trespass against us. And lead us not into temptation, but deliver us from evil. Amen.

People were bringing even infants to him that he might touch them. *Luke 18:15*

Hail Mary, full of grace, the Lord is with thee; blessed art thou among women, and blessed is the Fruit of thy womb, Jesus. Holy Mary, Mother of God, pray for us sinners, now and at the hour of our death. Amen.

"Lord, ... only say the word and my servant will be healed." *Matthew 8:8*

Hail Mary ...

"The blind regain their sight." *Luke 7:22*

Hail Mary ...

"The lame walk." *Luke 7:22*

Hail Mary ...

"Lepers are cleansed." *Luke 7:22*

Hail Mary ...

"The deaf hear." *Luke 7:22*

Hail Mary ...

"The dead are raised." *Luke 7:22*

Hail Mary ...

"The poor have the good news proclaimed to them." *Luke 7:22*

Hail Mary ...

"Ten were cleansed, were they not? Where are the other nine?" *Luke 17:17*

Hail Mary ...

"Has none but this [Samaritan] returned to give thanks to God?"

Luke 17:18

Hail Mary ...

Glory be to the Father, and to the Son, and to the Holy Spirit. As it was in the beginning, is now, and ever shall be, world without end. Amen.

O My Jesus, forgive us our sins, save us from the fires of Hell, lead all souls to Heaven, especially those who are in most need of Thy Mercy.

The Fourth Luminous Mystery
The Transfiguration

The mountain of the LORD's house shall be established as the highest mountain. *Isaiah 2:2*

Our Father, Who art in Heaven, hallowed be Thy Name. Thy kingdom come, Thy will be done on earth as it is in Heaven. Give us this day our daily bread, and forgive us our trespasses, as we forgive those who trespass against us. And lead us not into temptation, but deliver us from evil. Amen.

Jesus took Peter, James, and John ... up a high mountain. *Matthew 17:1*

Hail Mary, full of grace, the Lord is with thee; blessed art thou among women, and blessed is the Fruit of thy womb, Jesus. Holy Mary, Mother of God, pray for us sinners, now and at the hour of our death. Amen.

He was transfigured before them. *Matthew 17:2*

Hail Mary ...

His face shone like the sun. ... the bright morning star.
Matthew 17:2, Revelation 22:16

Hail Mary ...

His face shone like the sun at its brightest. ... rays shine forth. *Revelation 1:16, Habakkuk 3:4*

Hail Mary ...

His clothes became white as light. *Matthew 17:2*

Hail Mary ...

From the pillar of cloud God spoke. *Psalm 99:7*

Hail Mary ...

"This is my beloved Son." *Matthew 17:5*

Hail Mary ...

[The disciples] ... were very much afraid. *Matthew 17:6*

Hail Mary ...

"I am the light of the world. Whoever follows me will not walk in darkness." *John 8:12*

Hail Mary ...

O Most High, when I am afraid, in you I place my trust. *Psalm 56:3-4*

Hail Mary ...

Glory be to the Father, and to the Son, and to the Holy Spirit. As it was in the beginning, is now, and ever shall be, world without end. Amen.

O My Jesus, forgive us our sins, save us from the fires of Hell, lead all souls to Heaven, especially those who are in most need of Thy Mercy.

The Fifth Luminous Mystery
The Institution of the Eucharist

"Keep, then, this custom of the unleavened bread." *Exodus 12:17*

Our Father, Who art in Heaven, hallowed be Thy Name. Thy kingdom come, Thy will be done on earth as it is in Heaven. Give us this day our daily bread, and forgive us our trespasses, as we forgive those who trespass against us. And lead us not into temptation, but deliver us from evil. Amen.

On the first day of the Feast of the Unleavened Bread, ... [Jesus] took his place at table with the apostles. *Matthew 26:17, Luke 22:14*

Hail Mary, full of grace, the Lord is with thee; blessed art thou among women, and blessed is the Fruit of thy womb, Jesus. Holy Mary, Mother of God, pray for us sinners, now and at the hour of our death. Amen.

"My Father gives you the true bread from heaven." *John 6:32*

Hail Mary ...

Then he took the bread, said the blessing.
Luke 22:19

Hail Mary ...

"This is my body, which will be given for you."
Luke 22:19

Hail Mary ...

"The bread of God ... gives life to the world." *John 6:33*

Hail Mary ...

"This cup is … my blood, which will be shed for you." Luke 22:20

Hail Mary …

I will raise the cup of salvation and call on the name of the LORD. Psalm 116:13

Hail Mary …

"Do this in remembrance of me." 1 Corinthians 11:24

Hail Mary …

"You are a priest forever." … "Give us each day our daily bread." Psalm 110:4, Luke 11:3

Hail Mary …

They devoted themselves to … the breaking of the bread and to the prayers. Acts of the Apostles 2:42

Hail Mary …

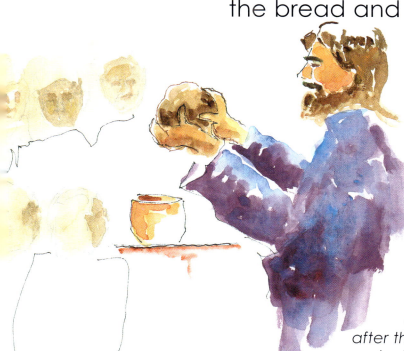

Glory be to the Father, and to the Son, and to the Holy Spirit. As it was in the beginning, is now, and ever shall be, world without end. Amen.

O My Jesus, forgive us our sins, save us from the fires of Hell, lead all souls to Heaven, especially those who are in most need of Thy Mercy.

Hail, holy Queen, Mother of mercy, our life, our sweetness and our hope. To thee do we cry, poor banished children of Eve! To thee do we send up our sighs, mourning and weeping in this valley of tears. Turn then, most gracious advocate, thine eyes of mercy towards us. And after this, our exile, show unto us the blessed Fruit of thy womb, Jesus. O clement, O loving, O sweet Virgin Mary.

V. Pray for us, O holy Mother of God,
R. That we may be made worthy of the promises of Christ.

The Sorrowful Mysteries

In the Name of the Father and of the Son and of the Holy Spirit. Amen.

I believe in God, the Father almighty, Creator of heaven and earth, and in Jesus Christ, his only Son, our Lord, who was conceived by the Holy Spirit, born of the Virgin Mary, suffered under Pontius Pilate, was crucified, died and was buried; he descended into hell; on the third day he rose again from the dead; he ascended into heaven, and is seated at the right hand of God the Father almighty; from there he will come to judge the living and the dead. I believe in the Holy Spirit, the holy catholic Church, the communion of saints, the forgiveness of sins, the resurrection of the body, and life everlasting. Amen.

May the Lord direct your hearts.

2 Thessalonians 3:5

Our Father, Who art in Heaven, hallowed be Thy Name. Thy kingdom come, Thy will be done on earth as it is in Heaven. Give us this day our daily bread, and forgive us our trespasses, as we forgive those who trespass against us. And lead us not into temptation, but deliver us from evil. Amen.

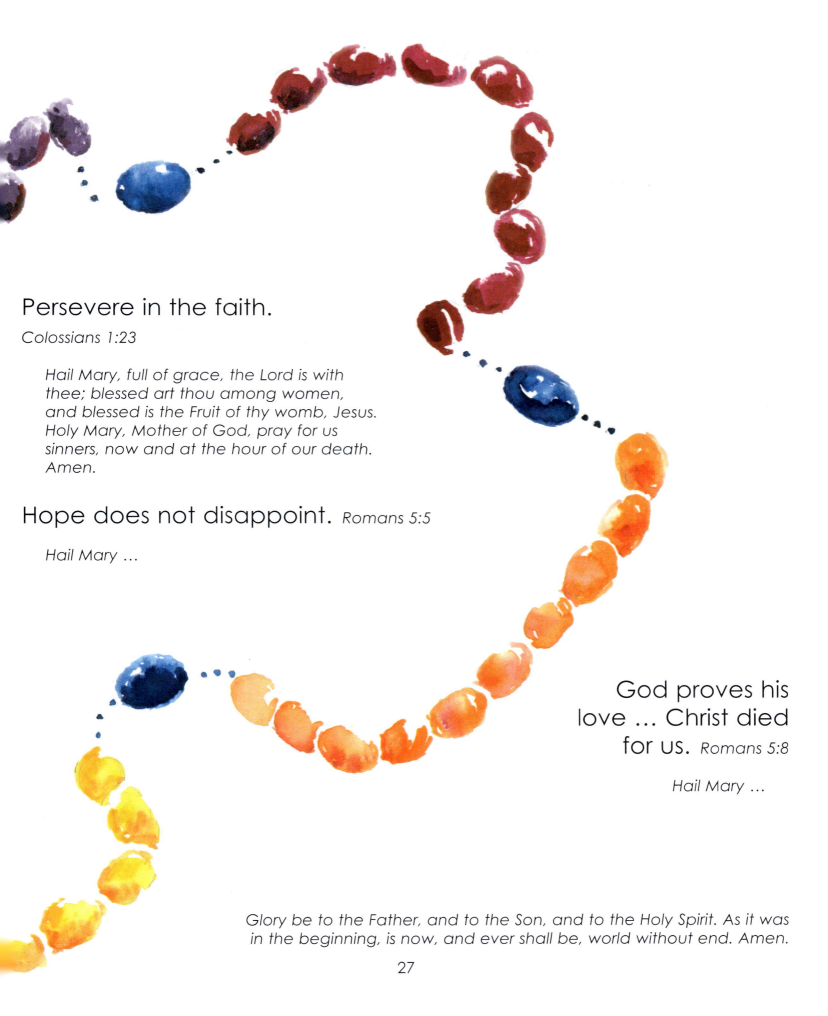

Persevere in the faith.
Colossians 1:23

Hail Mary, full of grace, the Lord is with thee; blessed art thou among women, and blessed is the Fruit of thy womb, Jesus. Holy Mary, Mother of God, pray for us sinners, now and at the hour of our death. Amen.

Hope does not disappoint. Romans 5:5

Hail Mary …

God proves his love … Christ died for us. Romans 5:8

Hail Mary …

Glory be to the Father, and to the Son, and to the Holy Spirit. As it was in the beginning, is now, and ever shall be, world without end. Amen.

The First Sorrowful Mystery
The Agony in the Garden

There was a garden. ... Gethsemane.

John 18:1, Matthew 26:36

Our Father, Who art in Heaven, hallowed be Thy Name. Thy kingdom come, Thy will be done on earth as it is in Heaven. Give us this day our daily bread, and forgive us our trespasses, as we forgive those who trespass against us. And lead us not into temptation, but deliver us from evil. Amen.

Is anyone among you suffering? ... Pray. *James 5:13*

Hail Mary, full of grace, the Lord is with thee; blessed art thou among women, and blessed is the Fruit of thy womb, Jesus. Holy Mary, Mother of God, pray for us sinners, now and at the hour of our death. Amen.

LORD, hear my prayer.

Psalm 143:1

Hail Mary ...

"My Father, if it is possible, let this cup pass from me; yet, not as I will, but as you will."

Matthew 26:39

Hail Mary ...

He was in such agony. *Luke 22:43*

Hail Mary ...

His sweat became like drops of blood falling on the ground. *Luke 22:44*

Hail Mary ...

To strengthen him an angel from heaven appeared to him. *Luke 22:43*

Hail Mary ...

Persevere in prayer. *Colossians 4:2*

Hail Mary ...

"Judas, are you betraying the Son of Man with a kiss?" *Luke 22:48*

Hail Mary ...

"At this I weep, my eyes run with tears." *Lamentations 1:16*

Hail Mary ...

[Jesus] became the source of eternal salvation for all who obey him. *Hebrews 5:9*

Hail Mary ...

Glory be to the Father, and to the Son, and to the Holy Spirit. As it was in the beginning, is now, and ever shall be, world without end. Amen.

O My Jesus, forgive us our sins, save us from the fires of Hell, lead all souls to Heaven, especially those who are in most need of Thy Mercy.

The Second Sorrowful Mystery
The Scourging at the Pillar

They spat in his face and struck him. *Matthew 26:67*

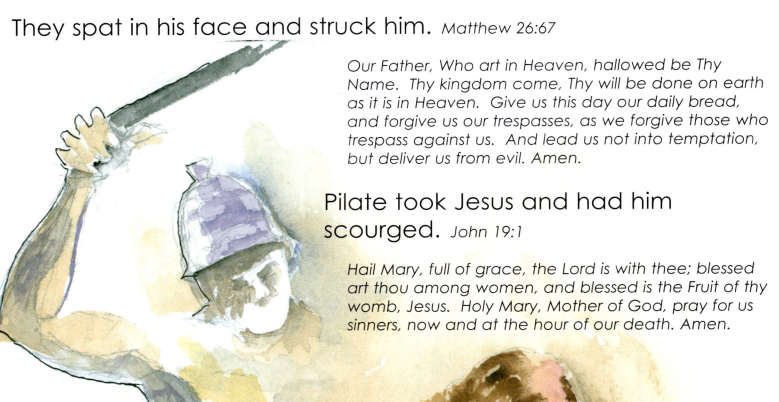

Our Father, Who art in Heaven, hallowed be Thy Name. Thy kingdom come, Thy will be done on earth as it is in Heaven. Give us this day our daily bread, and forgive us our trespasses, as we forgive those who trespass against us. And lead us not into temptation, but deliver us from evil. Amen.

Pilate took Jesus and had him scourged. *John 19:1*

Hail Mary, full of grace, the Lord is with thee; blessed art thou among women, and blessed is the Fruit of thy womb, Jesus. Holy Mary, Mother of God, pray for us sinners, now and at the hour of our death. Amen.

"This is my blood of the covenant which will be shed for many." *Mark 14:24*

Hail Mary ...

With the rod they strike on the cheek the ruler of Israel. *Micah 4:14*

Hail Mary ...

He left me desolate, in pain all day. *Lamentations 1:13*

Hail Mary ...

Deliver me from evildoers; from the bloodthirsty save me. *Psalm 59:3*

Hail Mary ...

How long, LORD? ... In crushing misfortune be patient. *Psalm 79:5, Sirach 2:4*

Hail Mary ...

He was pierced for our offenses, crushed for our sins. *Isaiah 53:5*

Hail Mary ...

Endure in affliction, persevere in prayer. *Romans 12:12*

Hail Mary ...

Blessed is the man who has patience and perseveres. *Daniel 12:12*

Hail Mary ...

God will rescue you. ... You shall not fear the terror of the night. *Psalm 91:3,5*

Hail Mary ...

Glory be to the Father, and to the Son, and to the Holy Spirit. As it was in the beginning, is now, and ever shall be, world without end. Amen.

O My Jesus, forgive us our sins, save us from the fires of Hell, lead all souls to Heaven, especially those who are in most need of Thy Mercy.

The Third Sorrowful Mystery
The Crowning of Thorns

"If you are the Messiah, tell us plainly." *John 10:24*

Our Father, Who art in Heaven, hallowed be Thy Name. Thy kingdom come, Thy will be done on earth as it is in Heaven. Give us this day our daily bread, and forgive us our trespasses, as we forgive those who trespass against us. And lead us not into temptation, but deliver us from evil. Amen.

Jesus answered them, "I told you and you do not believe."

John 10:25

Hail Mary, full of grace, the Lord is with thee; blessed art thou among women, and blessed is the Fruit of thy womb, Jesus. Holy Mary, Mother of God, pray for us sinners, now and at the hour of our death. Amen.

Even to the death fight for truth.

Sirach 4:28

Hail Mary …

Weaving a crown of thorns, [they] placed it on him. *Mark 15:17*

Hail Mary ...

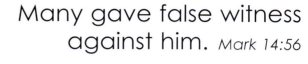

Many gave false witness against him. *Mark 14:56*

Hail Mary ...

If God is for us, who can be against us? *Romans 8:31*

Hail Mary ...

When he was insulted, he returned no insult. *1 Peter 2:23*

Hail Mary ...

Jesus was silent. *Matthew 26:63*

Hail Mary ...

You need endurance to do the will of God. *Hebrews 10:36*

Hail Mary ...

Love is patient. *1 Corinthians 13:4*

Hail Mary ...

Remain faithful until death. *Revelation-2:10*

Hail Mary ...

Glory be to the Father, and to the Son, and to the Holy Spirit. As it was in the beginning, is now, and ever shall be, world without end. Amen.

O My Jesus, forgive us our sins, save us from the fires of Hell, lead all souls to Heaven, especially those who are in most need of Thy Mercy.

The Fourth Sorrowful Mystery
The Carrying of the Cross

Oppressed and condemned, he was taken away. *Isaiah 53:8*

Our Father, Who art in Heaven, hallowed be Thy Name. Thy kingdom come, Thy will be done on earth as it is in Heaven. Give us this day our daily bread, and forgive us our trespasses, as we forgive those who trespass against us. And lead us not into temptation, but deliver us from evil. Amen.

A man's spirit sustains him in infirmity.
Proverbs 18:14

Hail Mary, full of grace, the Lord is with thee; blessed art thou among women, and blessed is the Fruit of thy womb, Jesus. Holy Mary, Mother of God, pray for us sinners, now and at the hour of our death. Amen.

A large crowd of people followed Jesus. *Luke 23:27*

Hail Mary ...

Though I have fallen, I will arise. *Micah 7:8*

Hail Mary ...

Bear one another's burdens. *Galatians 6:2*

Hail Mary ...

They pressed into service a passerby, Simon, ... to carry his cross. *Mark 15:21*

Hail Mary ...

"Come, follow me." *Mark 10:21*

Hail Mary ...

"Whoever follows me will not walk in darkness, but will have the light of life." *John 8:12*

Hail Mary ...

"Take my yoke upon you and learn from me, for I am meek and humble of heart." *Matthew 11:29*

Hail Mary ...

I have the strength for everything through him. *Philippians 4:13*

Hail Mary ...

The LORD, your God, shall you follow. *Deuteronomy 13:5*

Hail Mary ...

Glory be to the Father, and to the Son, and to the Holy Spirit. As it was in the beginning, is now, and ever shall be, world without end. Amen.

O My Jesus, forgive us our sins, save us from the fires of Hell, lead all souls to Heaven, especially those who are in most need of Thy Mercy.

The Fifth Sorrowful Mystery
The Crucifixion

The Place of the Skull, in Hebrew, Golgotha. There they crucified him. *John 19:17-18*

Our Father, Who art in Heaven, hallowed be Thy Name. Thy kingdom come, Thy will be done on earth as it is in Heaven. Give us this day our daily bread, and forgive us our trespasses, as we forgive those who trespass against us. And lead us not into temptation, but deliver us from evil. Amen.

"Father, forgive them." *Luke 23:34*

Hail Mary, full of grace, the Lord is with thee; blessed art thou among women, and blessed is the Fruit of thy womb, Jesus. Holy Mary, Mother of God, pray for us sinners, now and at the hour of our death. Amen.

[Jesus] said to the disciple, "Behold your mother." *John 19:27*

Hail Mary …

My God, my God, why have you abandoned me? *Psalm 22:2*

Hail Mary …

"Behold, the Lamb of God who takes away the sin of the world." *John 1:29*

Hail Mary …

He surrendered himself to death and was counted among the wicked. *Isaiah 53:12*

Hail Mary …

"Jesus, remember me." *Luke 23:42*

Hail Mary …

He pierces my sides … The thought of my homeless poverty is wormwood and gall. *Lamentations 3:13,19*

Hail Mary …

"Father, into your hands I commend my spirit." *Luke 23:46*

Hail Mary …

"It is finished." … We have redemption by his blood. *John 19:30, Ephesians 1:7*

Hail Mary …

"For God so loved the world that he gave his only Son, so that everyone who believes in him might not perish but might have eternal life." *John 3:16*

Hail Mary …

Glory be to the Father, and to the Son, and to the Holy Spirit. As it was in the beginning, is now, and ever shall be, world without end. Amen.

O My Jesus, forgive us our sins, save us from the fires of Hell, lead all souls to Heaven, especially those who are in most need of Thy Mercy.

Hail, holy Queen, Mother of mercy, our life, our sweetness and our hope. To thee do we cry, poor banished children of Eve! To thee do we send up our sighs, mourning and weeping in this valley of tears. Turn then, most gracious advocate, thine eyes of mercy towards us. And after this, our exile, show unto us the blessed Fruit of thy womb, Jesus. O clement, O loving, O sweet Virgin Mary.

V. Pray for us, O holy Mother of God,
R. That we may be made worthy of the promises of Christ.

The Glorious Mysteries

In the Name of the Father and of the Son and of the Holy Spirit. Amen.

I believe in God, the Father almighty, Creator of heaven and earth, and in Jesus Christ, his only Son, our Lord, who was conceived by the Holy Spirit, born of the Virgin Mary, suffered under Pontius Pilate, was crucified, died and was buried; he descended into hell; on the third day he rose again from the dead; he ascended into heaven, and is seated at the right hand of God the Father almighty; from there he will come to judge the living and the dead. I believe in the Holy Spirit, the holy catholic Church, the communion of saints, the forgiveness of sins, the resurrection of the body, and life everlasting. Amen.

Give glory, all you peoples! *Psalm 117:1-2*

Our Father, Who art in Heaven, hallowed be Thy Name. Thy kingdom come, Thy will be done on earth as it is in Heaven. Give us this day our daily bread, and forgive us our trespasses, as we forgive those who trespass against us. And lead us not into temptation, but deliver us from evil. Amen.

"If you believe you will see the glory of God." *John 11:40*

Hail Mary, full of grace, the Lord is with thee; blessed art thou among women, and blessed is the Fruit of thy womb, Jesus. Holy Mary, Mother of God, pray for us sinners, now and at the hour of our death. Amen.

We have set our hope on the living God.

1 Timothy 4:10

Hail Mary ...

Faith, hope, love ... the greatest of these is love.

1 Corinthians 13:13

Hail Mary ...

Glory be to the Father, and to the Son, and to the Holy Spirit. As it was in the beginning, is now, and ever shall be, world without end. Amen.

The First Glorious Mystery
The Resurrection

The depths of the abyss: who can explore these? *Sirach 1:3*

Our Father, Who art in Heaven, hallowed be Thy Name. Thy kingdom come, Thy will be done on earth as it is in Heaven. Give us this day our daily bread, and forgive us our trespasses, as we forgive those who trespass against us. And lead us not into temptation, but deliver us from evil. Amen.

Just as Jonah was in the belly of the whale three days and three nights, so will the Son of Man be in the heart of the earth. *Matthew 12:40*

Hail Mary, full of grace, the Lord is with thee; blessed art thou among women, and blessed is the Fruit of thy womb, Jesus. Holy Mary, Mother of God, pray for us sinners, now and at the hour of our death. Amen.

"I am the resurrection and the life." *John 11:25*

Hail Mary ...

Mary of Magdala went and announced to the disciples, "I have seen the Lord." *John 20:18*

Hail Mary ...

Peter got up and ran to the tomb. *Luke 24:12*

Hail Mary ...

I am the first and the last, the one who lives. *Revelation 1:17-18*

Hail Mary ...

[Depend] on faith to know him and the power of his resurrection. *Philippians 3:9-10*

Hail Mary ...

He is the living God, enduring forever.
Daniel 6:27

Hail Mary ...

"Look at my hands and feet, that it is I myself." *Luke 24:40*

Hail Mary ...

In life he performed wonders, and after death, marvelous deeds. *Sirach 48:14*

Hail Mary ...

"I am the bread of life." *John 6:35*

Hail Mary ...

Glory be to the Father, and to the Son, and to the Holy Spirit. As it was in the beginning, is now, and ever shall be, world without end. Amen.

O My Jesus, forgive us our sins, save us from the fires of Hell, lead all souls to Heaven, especially those who are in most need of Thy Mercy.

The Second Glorious Mystery
The Ascension

"I am leaving the world and going back to the Father." *John 16:28*

Our Father, Who art in Heaven, hallowed be Thy Name. Thy kingdom come, Thy will be done on earth as it is in Heaven. Give us this day our daily bread, and forgive us our trespasses, as we forgive those who trespass against us. And lead us not into temptation, but deliver us from evil. Amen.

When I am lifted up from the earth, I will draw everyone to myself. *John 12:32*

Hail Mary, full of grace, the Lord is with thee; blessed art thou among women, and blessed is the Fruit of thy womb, Jesus. Holy Mary, Mother of God, pray for us sinners, now and at the hour of our death. Amen.

"I will never forsake you or abandon you." *Hebrews 13:5*

Hail Mary …

The Lord Jesus … was taken up into heaven and took his seat at the right hand of God.

Mark 16:19

Hail Mary …

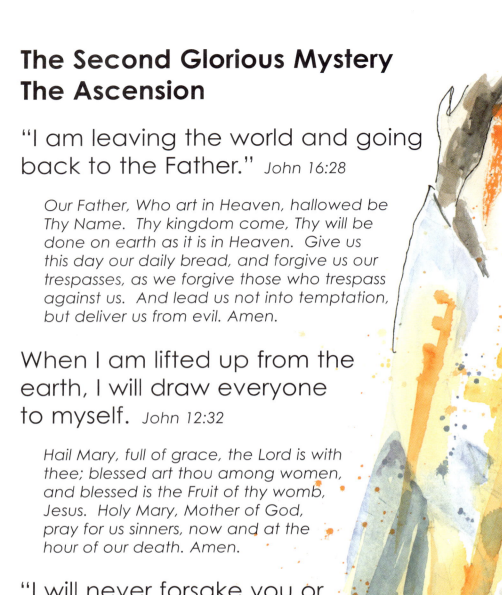

God's grandeur is beyond understanding. *Psalm 145:3*

Hail Mary ...

From heaven the LORD looks down and observes the whole human race. *Psalm 33:13*

Hail Mary ...

In the highest heavens did I dwell, my throne on a pillar of cloud. *Sirach 24:4*

Hail Mary ...

"I will come back again and take you to myself." *John 14:3*

Hail Mary ...

The LORD is exalted, enthroned on high. *Isaiah 33:5*

Hail Mary ...

Your throne shall stand firm forever. *2 Samuel 7:16*

Hail Mary ...

"Jesus ... will return in the same way as you have seen him going into heaven." *Acts of the Apostles 1:11*

Hail Mary ...

Glory be to the Father, and to the Son, and to the Holy Spirit. As it was in the beginning, is now, and ever shall be, world without end. Amen.

O My Jesus, forgive us our sins, save us from the fires of Hell, lead all souls to Heaven, especially those who are in most need of Thy Mercy.

The Third Glorious Mystery
The Descent of the Holy Spirit

You make the winds your messengers; flaming fire, your ministers.

Psalm 104:4

Our Father, Who art in Heaven, hallowed be Thy Name. Thy kingdom come, Thy will be done on earth as it is in Heaven. Give us this day our daily bread, and forgive us our trespasses, as we forgive those who trespass against us. And lead us not into temptation, but deliver us from evil. Amen.

There appeared to them tongues as of fire, which parted and came to rest on each of them.

Acts of the Apostles 2:3

Hail Mary, full of grace, the Lord is with thee; blessed art thou among women, and blessed is the Fruit of thy womb, Jesus. Holy Mary, Mother of God, pray for us sinners, now and at the hour of our death. Amen.

They were all filled with the holy Spirit.

Acts of the Apostles 2:4

Hail Mary ...

I am filled with power, with the spirit of the LORD.

Micah 3:8

Hail Mary ...

Every spirit that acknowledges Jesus Christ come in the flesh belongs to God. *1 John 4:2*

Hail Mary ...

The community of believers was of one heart and one mind. *Acts of the Apostles 4:32*

Hail Mary ...

"Go therefore, and make disciples of all nations."
Matthew 28:19

Hail Mary ...

Proclaim the word. ... Perform the work of an evangelist.
2 Timothy 4:2,5

Hail Mary ...

Pray in the holy Spirit. *Jude 20*

Hail Mary ...

God is Spirit. ... Worship in Spirit and truth. *John 4:24*

Hail Mary ...

The fruit of the Spirit is love, joy, peace.
Galatians 5:22

Hail Mary ...

Glory be to the Father, and to the Son, and to the Holy Spirit. As it was in the beginning, is now, and ever shall be, world without end. Amen.

O My Jesus, forgive us our sins, save us from the fires of Hell, lead all souls to Heaven, especially those who are in most need of Thy Mercy.

The Fourth Glorious Mystery
The Assumption of the Blessed Virgin Mary into Heaven

Seek first the kingdom [of God]. *Matthew 6:33*

Our Father, Who art in Heaven, hallowed be Thy Name. Thy kingdom come, Thy will be done on earth as it is in Heaven. Give us this day our daily bread, and forgive us our trespasses, as we forgive those who trespass against us. And lead us not into temptation, but deliver us from evil. Amen.

The LORD bless you and ... let his face shine upon you.
Numbers 6:24-25

Hail Mary, full of grace, the Lord is with thee; blessed art thou among women, and blessed is the Fruit of thy womb, Jesus. Holy Mary, Mother of God, pray for us sinners, now and at the hour of our death. Amen.

Remain faithful until death, and I will give you the crown of life.
Revelation 2:10

Hail Mary ...

The one who perseveres to the end will be saved. *Matthew 24:13*

Hail Mary ...

Let us reach out our hearts toward God in heaven! *Lamentations 3:41*

Hail Mary ...

"Arise, my beloved, my beautiful one." *Song of Songs 2:10*

Hail Mary ...

You have eternal life, you who believe in the name of the Son of God. *1 John 5:13*

Hail Mary ...

Mary said: …
"He has … lifted up the lowly."
Luke 1:46,52

Hail Mary …

"Blessed are the clean of heart, for they will see God." *Matthew 5:8*

Hail Mary …

I give them eternal life. *John 10:28*

Hail Mary …

Your life is hidden with Christ in God.
Colossians 3:3

Hail Mary …

Glory be to the Father, and to the Son, and to the Holy Spirit. As it was in the beginning, is now, and ever shall be, world without end. Amen.

O My Jesus, forgive us our sins, save us from the fires of Hell, lead all souls to Heaven, especially those who are in most need of Thy Mercy.

The Fifth Glorious Mystery
The Coronation of Mary, Queen of Heaven and Earth

"The Father will honor whoever serves me." ... Honor ... your mother. *John 12:26, Exodus 20:12*

Our Father, Who art in Heaven, hallowed be Thy Name. Thy kingdom come, Thy will be done on earth as it is in Heaven. Give us this day our daily bread, and forgive us our trespasses, as we forgive those who trespass against us. And lead us not into temptation, but deliver us from evil. Amen.

Mary said: ... "Behold, from now on will all ages call me blessed." *Luke 1:46,48*

Hail Mary, full of grace, the Lord is with thee; blessed art thou among women, and blessed is the Fruit of thy womb, Jesus. Holy Mary, Mother of God, pray for us sinners, now and at the hour of our death. Amen.

"The righteous will shine like the sun in the kingdom of their Father." *Matthew 13:43*

Hail Mary ...

This is the promise that he made us: eternal life. *1 John 2:25*

Hail Mary ...

A great sign appeared in the sky, a woman [with] a crown of twelve stars. *Revelation 12:1*

Hail Mary ...

"Whoever humbles himself will be exalted." *Matthew 23:12*

Hail Mary ...

He who sows virtue has a sure reward. *Proverbs 11:18*

Hail Mary ...

"Rejoice ... your reward will be great in heaven." *Matthew 5:12*

Hail Mary ...

Whoever does the will of God remains forever.
1 John 2:17

Hail Mary ...

Bless the LORD who has crowned you with glory!
Sirach 45:26

Hail Mary ...

Pray for us, too, that God may open a door to us.
Colossians 4:3

Hail Mary ...

Glory be to the Father, and to the Son, and to the Holy Spirit. As it was in the beginning, is now, and ever shall be, world without end. Amen.

O My Jesus, forgive us our sins, save us from the fires of Hell, lead all souls to Heaven, especially those who are in most need of Thy Mercy.

Hail, holy Queen, Mother of mercy, our life, our sweetness and our hope. To thee do we cry, poor banished children of Eve! To thee do we send up our sighs, mourning and weeping in this valley of tears. Turn then, most gracious advocate, thine eyes of mercy towards us. And after this, our exile, show unto us the blessed Fruit of thy womb, Jesus. O clement, O loving, O sweet Virgin Mary.

V. Pray for us, O holy Mother of God,
R. That we may be made worthy of the promises of Christ.

The Books of the Bible

The Old Testament

Genesis
Exodus
Leviticus
Numbers
Deuteronomy
Joshua
Judges
Ruth
1 Samuel
2 Samuel
1 Kings
2 Kings
1 Chronicles
2 Chronicles
Ezra
Nehemiah
Tobit
Judith
Esther
1 Maccabees
2 Maccabees
Job
Psalm
Proverbs
Ecclesiastes
Song of Songs
Wisdom

Sirach
Isaiah
Jeremiah
Lamentations
Baruch
Ezekiel
Daniel
Hosea
Joel
Amos
Obadiah
Jonah
Micah
Nahum
Habakkuk
Zephaniah
Haggai
Zechariah
Malachi

The New Testament

Matthew
Mark
Luke
John
Acts of the Apostles
Romans
1 Corinthians
2 Corinthians
Galatians
Ephesians
Philippians
Colossians
1 Thessalonians
2 Thessalonians
1 Timothy
2 Timothy
Titus
Philemon
Hebrews
James
1 Peter
2 Peter
1 John
2 John
3 John
Jude
Revelation

For Teachers and Parents

Frequently Asked Questions

What is the Most Holy Rosary?

The Most Holy Rosary combines mental prayer with vocal prayer. We meditate on the sacred mysteries of the life, death, and glory of Jesus Christ and His Blessed Mother, while we, simultaneously, pray decades of prayers. Each decade consists of one *Our Father* and ten *Hail Marys*. The decade concludes with a *Glory Be* and *The Fatima Prayer (O My Jesus)*.

How is the 2nd Edition of this prayer book different from the 1st Edition?

For many centuries, the Most Holy Rosary consisted of fifteen decades in three groups of mysteries – the Joyful, Sorrowful, and the Glorious. In the Apostolic Letter *Rosarium Virginis Mariae (Oct, 2002)*, Pope Blessed John Paul II recommended praying an additional set of mysteries, called the Luminous Mysteries. These Mysteries of Light reflect on Christ's public ministry. This 2nd edition includes these Luminous Mysteries on pages 14-25 and also includes a Study Guide on pages 54-57.

What are the Sacred Mysteries of the Rosary?

The mysteries are organized into four groups: Joyful, Luminous, Sorrowful, and Glorious.

>The Joyful Mysteries *(The Annunciation, The Visitation, The Nativity, The Presentation of Jesus in the Temple, and The Finding of Jesus in the Temple)* remind us of the early life of Jesus.

>The Luminous Mysteries *(The Baptism of Jesus, The Wedding at Cana, The Proclamation of the Kingdom, The Transfiguration, and The Institution of the Eucharist)* reveal the public ministry of Jesus Christ.

>The Sorrowful Mysteries *(The Agony in the Garden, The Scourging at the Pillar, The Crowning of Thorns, The Carrying of the Cross, and The Crucifixion)* allow us to reflect on the passion and death of Christ.

>The Glorious Mysteries *(The Resurrection, The Ascension, The Descent of the Holy Spirit, The Assumption of the Blessed Virgin Mary into Heaven, and The Coronation of the Blessed Virgin Mary, Queen of Heaven and Earth)* bring us to a realization of the mission of Jesus Christ fulfilled - calling all of us to eternal life.

What is a Scriptural Rosary?

A Scriptural Rosary responds to the words from the Catechism of the Catholic Church. "Prayer should accompany the reading of Sacred Scripture, so that a dialogue takes place between God and man." *(CCC 2653)* Pope Blessed John Paul II said the Rosary is "A prayer so easy and yet so rich [that it] deserves to be rediscovered … Rediscover the Rosary in the light of Scripture."

A Scriptural Rosary simplifies, yet spiritually edifies, the mental prayer in the Most Holy Rosary. A Scriptural Rosary is a conversation with God. He speaks to us through His Word and we respond with the *Our Father*, or the Angelic salutation, the *Hail Mary*. Sacred Scriptures are added to the praying of the Most Holy Rosary to keep us alert, to help us understand the mysteries, and to converse with God in the presence of His Blessed Mother.

An example of this meditative conversation would be to join Mary at the foot of the cross and hear Jesus speak His last words during the Crucifixion as seen on pages 36-37.

Why not pray in our own words, rather than using a set prayer such as the Rosary?

Actually, praying the Rosary is our own, individualized prayer. Each Rosary prayed devotedly is unique and special to Jesus and Mary. While the main prayers of the Rosary are set, they are in St. Thomas Aquinas' words, "the three greatest prayers." *The Apostles' Creed* is handed down to us from Jesus' twelve Apostles and lists the beliefs of our faith. The Lord's Prayer, the *Our Father*, is the perfect prayer that Jesus taught us to pray to His Father. The Angelic Salutation, coupled with words from the Catholic Church, comprises the *Hail Mary*. Thus, we echo the Archangel Gabriel's greeting of honor to the "most blessed among women." Through mental prayer, meditation on the mysteries, we focus our personal prayer of veneration, petition, intercession or thanksgiving. Indeed, the Rosary is a universal prayer for the individual.

How do I pray the Rosary?

While holding the Crucifix in your right hand, make the *Sign of the Cross* and recite the *Apostles' Creed*.

On the first bead, recite the *Our Father*. On the following three small beads, recite the *Hail Mary* for an increase in the three virtues of faith, hope, and love. Next, pray the *Glory Be*.

For each decade, identify the mystery and meditate on the mystery; then recite on the larger bead the *Our Father*. On each of the ten small beads, recite the *Hail Mary*, keeping in mind an aspect of the mystery. Recite the *Glory Be*, followed by *The Fatima Prayer (O My Jesus)*. Repeat this for five decades and conclude by praying the *Hail Holy Queen*.

Additionally, the following prayer can be said after the Hail Holy Queen.

Prayer after the Rosary

> O God, whose only begotten Son, by His life, death and resurrection, has purchased for us the rewards of eternal life; grant, we beseech Thee, that, by meditating upon these mysteries of the Most Holy Rosary of the Blessed Virgin Mary, we may imitate what they contain and obtain what they promise, through the same Christ our Lord. Amen.
>
> May the divine assistance remain always with us. And may the souls of the faithful departed, through the mercy of God, rest in peace. Amen.

While a complete Rosary consists in praying all twenty mysteries, it is more typical of group prayer to only pray five decades or mysteries at a time. For school opening prayer or introducing the Rosary to young children, you may be inclined to only pray one mystery. A five or twenty decade Rosary may be too daunting for a very young child, but a one decade Rosary with a Bible lesson about the particular mystery brings the melody of prayer alive with mental pictures of persons, places, and events.

Is there a set pattern in which to pray the mysteries?

Generally, the Joyful Mysteries are prayed on Monday and Thursday, the Sorrowful on Tuesday and Friday, and the Glorious on Wednesday, Saturday, and Sunday. However, during the Sundays of the Christmas season, pray the Joyful Mysteries, and during the Sundays of Lent, pray the Sorrowful Mysteries. With the addition of the Luminous Mysteries, Pope Blessed John Paul II recommended that the Joyful Mysteries be prayed on Saturday, instead of the Glorious, and the Luminous Mysteries on Thursday.

What is a source of information about the Rosary, especially its origins and traditions?

The best way to learn more about this Marian devotion is to read St. Louis de Montfort's devotional classic, <u>The Secret of the Rosary.</u> Additionally, the Study Guide on pages 54-57 provides a table of information and questions to challenge you to a deeper study of the mysteries of the Rosary and Sacred Scriptures.

How did the idea for Speak, Lord, I am Listening originate?

In the early 1990s, after teaching a tenth grade CCD class which integrated the fifteen mysteries of the Rosary into the Bible Study course curriculum, Christine Haapala, the author, thought *"Is there a connection between the 150 Psalms and 150 Hail Marys of the Rosary?"* While the formal method of praying the Rosary is credited to St. Dominic, the origins of the Most Holy Rosary date more than a millennium and tradition roots it in the praying of the 150 Psalms. By replacing the Psalm prayers with the *Pater Noster* and the *Ave Maria* and counting the prayers on cords of 50 beads, the laity who could not read the Psalms and had no access to an expensive Bible could imitate the holiness of the monks of the Abbeys. Based on the connection to the Psalms, the Rosary has been called the Psalter of Jesus and Mary.

Based on this inspiration, the author expanded this concept and published her first book <u>From Genesis to Revelation: Seven Scriptural Rosaries</u> (Christendom Press, 1996). Since then, she has continued to write other books and newspaper articles. In the summer of the Jubilee Year, she started <u>Speak, Lord, I am Listening</u> and it was published in June, 2001. The book is designed to introduce, teach, and share the beauty of the mysteries of the Rosary with young children.

How did the artist and author come to collaborate on this project?

The author and Gus Muller, the artist, are members of the same parish, Holy Spirit Catholic Church, Annandale, Virginia. Gus Muller painted a watercolor depicting his interpretation of the Church at the beginning of the new millennium. He donated the painting to an auction, the benefits of which helped sponsor a parish youth group trip to Rome, where they had an audience with the Holy Father. The millennium painting prompted the author to ask the artist to create the illustrations for this book. Gus Muller stated that painting the pictures was a peaceful, joyous experience and that "with each mark of the pencil and stroke of the paintbrush, there seemed to be an additional hand guiding the movement."

Can you tell me more about Gus Muller and his work?

After retiring from a civil engineering career, Gus Muller fulfilled a life long desire to study art and paint seriously. It wasn't long before he discovered his interest and talent for watercolors and in the creative effects he could achieve with the medium's transparent paints. For the past 16 years, he has specialized in landscapes, seascapes, florals and portraits, many of which are displayed in various locations in Virginia, Maryland, and New Jersey. In the late 1990s, he did paintings of Mother Theresa and the Blessed Mother, and a painting of Holy Spirit Church which were auctioned to benefit his parish's Knights of Columbus chapter. His work is in a studio in Occoquan, Virginia.

Have Christine and Gus collaborated on other projects?

<u>Follow Me</u> is a Scriptural Stations of the Cross meditation prayer book for children. Christine wrote the book and Gus illustrated it in a similar fashion as this rosary book. In addition to illustrating each Station of the Cross, Gus also created a portrait watercolor of over 15 extraordinarily holy people. Each person was included with a particular Station of the Cross. While meditating on the sufferings of Christ, both children and adults, can see examples of holiness and understand what it means to be called to holiness. Pope Blessed John Paul II either canonized or beatified each of the people featured in this Stations of the Cross book.

Can you tell us more about the Catholic publishing company, Suffering Servant Scriptorium?

Founded in the Jubliee Year, Suffering Servant Scriptorium's mission is to substantially contribute to the increase in the prayer life of Catholics by distribution and publishing quality manuscripts and recordings. more information about the company and products can be found at the website www.sufferingservant.com. Also, a product list can be found on the last page of this book.

A STUDY AND D
The Joyful Mysteries

Mysteries	The Annunciation	The Visitation	The Nativity	The Presentation of Jesus in the Temple	The Finding of Jesus in the Temple
Where in the Bible is this Mystery?	Luke 1:26-38	Luke 1:39-80	Matthew 2:1-12 Luke 2:1-20	Luke 2:22-38	Luke 2:41-52
Jesus and the Blessed Virgin Mary	Mary humbly says Yes when asked if she would be the mother of Jesus, the Son of God	Mary shares her Son with others	The Holy Family - a model to be imitated	Mary thanks God for the gift of her Son - salvation of the world	For three days Mary and St. Joseph look for Jesus and find Him in His Father's house
Other Important People	St. Gabriel, the Archangel and St. Joseph	St. Elizabeth, Zechariah, and their son John (later known as St. John the Baptist)	St. Joseph, the Shepherds, and the Three Wise Men (Magi)	Anna and Simeon	Teachers
General Discussion Questions	What did God ask Mary to do? How is God calling us to serve Him? Like Mary, have we answered Yes to God's call?	Why did Mary go to visit her cousin St. Elizabeth for three months? Have we recently helped others, especially those in need?	What did the Wise Men bring to honor Jesus? Have you given to the poor? What are the spiritual and corporal works of mercy?	What gifts did Mary and St. Joseph bring to the temple? Do we find the time to thank God for all the blessings that He has given us?	What was Jesus doing when Mary and St. Joseph found Him? Do we spend time learning about God - the Father, the Son, and the Holy Spirit?
Watercolor Discussion Questions	Who was sent from God? What do we think the dove above St. Gabriel's hand means?	Who does Mary's veil remind us of? What important work did she do?	Who is the "Light of the World"? What animal helped Mary get to Bethlehem?	Why did Mary and St. Joseph take Jesus to the Temple? What was Simeon's prophecy and when was it fulfilled?	Mary and St. Joseph were worried while they looked for Jesus for three days. Do we ever make our family worry when we go somewhere without asking first?
Virtues to Imitate	Trust, Purity, and Humility	Service to and Love of Neighbor	Love of God, Joy, and Peace	Obedience	Gift of Understanding, Knowledge, and Wisdom

CUSSION GUIDE
The Luminous Mysteries

Mysteries	The Baptism of Jesus	The Wedding at Cana	The Proclamation of the Kingdom	The Transfiguration	The Institution of the Eucharist
Where in the Bible is this Mystery?	Matthew 3:13-17 Mark 1:9-11 Luke 3:21-22 John 1:29-34	John 2:1-11	Matthew 4:17 Matthew 4:23-5:12	Matthew 17:1-8 Mark 9:2-8 Luke 9:28-36	Matthew 26:26-29 Mark 14:22-25 Luke 22:14-20
Jesus and the Blessed Virgin Mary	Jesus is baptized pleasing God the Father	Jesus' first miracle in obedience to His Blessed Mother's request to serve others	Jesus' ministry increases; Jesus heals; Jesus teaches the Beatitudes; Jesus saves His people	Jesus reveals a glimpse of eternity through His glorified Body	Jesus shares the Passover Meal with His Apostles before His Passion
Other Important People	St. John the Baptist	Chief Stewart and servants	All who were cured by Jesus or heard Jesus speak	Moses and Elijah	The 12 Apostles
General Discussion Questions	What did God the Father say when Jesus was baptized? Who was there when we were baptized?	What did Jesus do when Mary asked Him to help? Do we obey our parents when they ask us to do something, even though it may not be what we want to do right now?	What are the Beatitudes? Do we know any stories or parables that Jesus told?	How did Jesus change? What are some of the glimpses of the spectacular beauty around us - God's creation - the Universe, the Sun, the moon, rainbows - name some others - what about your family?	Do we attend Mass every Sunday? Do we attend Mass at other times to show God we love Him?
Watercolor Discussion Questions	Who is the Dove? Who baptized Jesus?	What did Jesus tell the servants to fill the jars up with? What did it turn into?	Thousands of people listened to Jesus teach the good news. Do we spend time listening to the Word of God? God the Father forgave the sins of many people because they asked for forgiveness from His Son. Do we ask God's forgiveness when we have done something wrong?	Who are the two men that are with Jesus? What did these men do?	Who are the men gathered around Jesus? What is the Priest asking God to do to the bread and wine?
Virtues to Imitate	Purity	Fidelity	Sorrow for Sin	Courage	Love of the Eucharistic Lord and Adoration

A STUDY AND
The Sorrowful Mysteries

Mysteries	The Agony in the Garden	The Scourging at the Pillar	The Crowning of Thorns	The Carrying of the Cross	The Crucifixion
Where in the Bible is this Mystery?	Matthew 26:36-50 Mark 14:32-45 Luke 22:39-48	John 19:1	Matthew 27:27-31 Mark 15:16-20 John 19:2-3	Matthew 27:32 Mark 15:21 Luke 23:26-31 Luke 2:22-38	Matthew 27:33-54 Mark 15:22-39 Luke 23:33-47 John 19:18-37
Jesus and the Blessed Virgin Mary	During an evening of agony and profound prayer, Jesus accepts the will of His Father.	Jesus is flogged by the Romans	Jesus is mocked by the Roman Soldiers	Mary sees her Son struggling on the Via Dolorosa	Mary is at the Foot of the Cross - Jesus gives us Mary as Our Mother when He says "Behold thy Mother."
Other Important People	Peter and Judas	Pilate	Roman Soldiers	Simon of Cyrene and St. Veronica	St. Mary Magdalene, St. Dismas (the Good Thief), the Centurion, and St. John
General Discussion Questions	While Jesus was praying, who was sleeping? Who betrayed Jesus and how was he betrayed? When our friends hurt us, do we forgive them?	If there is suffering in our lives, do we give this to Jesus as a special sacrifice or offering?	What three things did the Roman Soldiers give to Jesus to mock Him? Do we ever make fun of others?	Who helped Jesus carry the cross? Would you be willing to help someone even when it is not the popular thing to do?	Who were the two people also crucified with Jesus Christ? What did Jesus promise one of them?
Watercolor Discussion Questions	Jesus is kneeling and praying to God the Father. What is Jesus praying for? Who gives Jesus strength?	Jesus suffered much for us, how do we thank Him? Who else suffered with Jesus?	Jesus is the King of Kings and Prince of Peace, how do we give Him honor and glory?	Jesus fell three times while carrying his cross, each time He got back up and kept going without complaint. God gives each of us a cross to carry, are we carrying it without complaint?	What do the letters INRI on the top of the cross mean?
Virtues to Imitate	Prayer, Meditation, and Contemplation	Prudence	Honesty	Patience	Final Perseverance

CUSSION GUIDE
The Glorious Mysteries

Mysteries	The Resurrection	The Ascension	The Descent of the Holy Spirit	The Assumption of the Blessed Virgin Mary into Heaven	The Coronation of the Blessed Virgin Mary, Queen of Heaven and Earth
Where in the Bible is this Mystery?	Matthew 28:1-10 Mark 16:1-11 Luke 24:1-12 John 20:1-18	Mark 16:19-20 Luke 24:50-51 Acts of the Apostles 1:6-11	Acts of the Apostles 2:1-4	Luke 1:52	Revelation 12:1-5
Jesus and the Blessed Virgin Mary	Jesus rises of His own power from the dead.	Jesus rises of His own power to the right hand of God the Father	Jesus promised to send the Paraclete, God the Holy Spirit	God assumes Mary, body and soul, to Heaven	Mary is honored above all mankind - for all nations shall call her blessed
Other Important People	St. Mary Magdalene, St. Peter, and St. John	The Apostles and others	The Apostles and others	Angels and Saints	The Church Triumphant
General Discussion Questions	Who did Jesus appear to after He rose from the dead? Are we looking for the Lord at all times, even though sometimes He seems to be far away?	After Jesus ascended to His Father, what did the angel tell his Apostles? Are you patiently waiting for Jesus' return?	What did the Apostles/Disciples do after they received the Holy Spirit? How do we share our faith with others?	Do we pray every day? Does the Mother of God have a special place in our prayer life? When our parents or grandparents want us to pray with them, do we do so willingly?	Do we show special honor to Mary throughout the year, by participating in events, such as, May Crownings or First Saturday Mass?
Watercolor Discussion Questions	Who is pictured along with Jesus? How does he serve the Church?	Who witnessed the Ascension?	What are the gifts of the Holy Spirit? Do we use these gifts in honor of Our Lord?	Who is Our Lady of Fatima? Who are the three children?	Do we know the story of Our Lady of Guadalupe?
Virtues to Imitate	Faith	Hope	Fortitude, Courage, and Zeal	Piety	Honor of Mary

Other Titles available from Suffering Servant Scriptorium

Prayer Books

Follow Me Inspired watercolors and selections of God's Word introduce children to the suffering of our Savior Jesus Christ by walking each step with Him to Calvary. Along with each station is a heroically holy person who epitomized self-sacrifice, and, primary, lived and died in the last century. Each were either beatified or canonized by Pope Blessed John Paul II.

Seraphim and Cherubim A Scriptural Chaplet of the Holy Angels. Angels have been with us since the beginning in the "Garden of Eden" and will be with us at the "End of Age." This prayer book joins together Sacred Scripture selections with special invocations to our Blessed Mother and the Holy Archangels. This book includes fabulous full-color pictures from the masters, such as, Raphael, Bruegel the Elder, Perugino and many others. It also includes a newly composed Novena of the Holy Angels and the traditional Litany of the Holy Angels. Those who pray without ceasing and ponder the Good News will find this book equally inspiring and encouraging.

In His Presence This book of meditations outlines SEVEN VISITS to the Blessed Sacrament. This prayer book can be used in one evening, such as, during the Holy Thursday Seven Church Pilgrimage. It can be used for seven consecutive days for a special prayer request. And, it can be used periodically, whenever you can spend time visiting Jesus in the Blessed Sacrament. This prayer book includes illustrations from Dante's Divine Comedy from the inspired artistry of the 19th centry Catholic illustrator Gusave Dóre.

His Sorrowful Passion This prayer book integrates Sacred Scripture meditations with the prayers of the Chaplet of Divine Mercy. There are two Scriptural Chaplets: one chronicles Jesus' Passion and the other features the Seven Penitential Psalms. The woodcuts of the 15th century Catholic artist, Albrecht Durer, illustrate this book.

The Suffering Servant's Courage (2nd Ed. with Luminous Mysteries) This prayer book integrates poignant Sacred Scripture verses about courage and fortitude, the prayers of the Most Holy Rosary, and illustrations from the inspired artistry of the 19th century Catholic illustrator Gustave Dóre.

Psalter of Jesus and Mary This pocket-size Scriptural Rosary prayer book includes the 150 Psalms Scriptural Rosary for the Joyful, Sorrowful and Glorious Mysteries and meditations for the Luminous Mysteries from the Book of Proverbs, the wise words of Solomon. The 20 Mysteries of the Most Holy Rosary open with a New Testament reflection. There is a short Scripture meditation from either Psalms or Proverbs for each Hail Mary. An Old and New Testament icon from Julius Schnorr von Carolsfeld's Treasury of Bible Illustrations accompany each mystery.

From Genesis to Revelation: Seven Scriptural Rosaries This prayer book is the most thorough and extensive collection of Scriptural Rosaries you will find anywhere. This prayer book goes well beyond the traditional Scriptural Rosary and penetrates the heart of the meditative spirit of the mysteries. It addresses many dimensions: time, from the Old to the New Testament; authors, from Moses, Isaiah, to the Evangelists; and perspectives, form the purely historical to deeper spiritual and prayerful insights. Those who pray the Rosary and those who read the Bible will equally find this prayer book inspirational.

Recorded Prayers available on CD

The Sanctity of Life Scriptural Rosary (2nd Ed. with Luminous Mysteries) Sacred Scripture selections prayed with the Most Holy Rosary uniquely brings you God's message of the dignity and sanctity of life. The prayers are accompanied by meditative piano music. Four different readers lead you in more than two hours of prayerful meditations. Includes four songs from the composer and soprano Nancy Scimone, winner of the UNITY Awards 2002 Best Sacramental Album of the Year for ORA PRO NOBIS. Includes 16-page book with the complete text of the Sacred Scripture selections. Double CD. CD 1 includes the Joyful and Luminous Mysteries and CD 2 includes the Sorrowful and Glorious Mysteries.

Time for Mercy Composer and singer Nancy Scimone offers you a new, spiritually uplifting Chaplet of Divine Mercy melody. This Scriptural Chaplet of Divine Mercy is based on the Penitential Psalm Scriptural Chaplet of Divine Mercy from the book, His Sorrowful Passion. Brother Leonard Konopka, MIC, prays selections from the Seven Penitential Psalms, while Nancy Scimone's crystal clear soprano voice brings us God's message of Divine Mercy and Infinite Grace. The CD includes the meditation song, "Thy Heart Immaculate", which was inspired by Saint Faustina who wrote in her Diary that the Blessed Virgin Mary said "I am not only the Queen of Heaven, but also the Mother of Mercy." *(Diary, 330)*

To purchase additional copies of this book or the works mentioned above, please visit your local Catholic bookstore. Individual orders or quantity discounts are also available by calling us at 888-652-9494. For more detailed information about these products and Suffering Servant Scriptorium and to listen to selections of the music and prayers, please visit www.sufferingservant.com.